DORLING KINDERSLEY

Astronauta:

La vida en el espacio

Escrito por Kate Hayden

Un libro de Dorling Kindersley

LONDON, NEW YORK, SYDNEY, DELHI, PARIS,
MUNICH, and JOHANNESBURG
dk.com

For Dorling Kindersley
Project Editor Louise Pritchard
Art Editor Jill Plank

Senior Editor Linda Esposito
Senior Art Editor Diane Thistlethwaite
US Editor Regina Kahney
Production Melanie Dowland
Picture Researcher Andrea Sadler
Illustrator Peter Dennis
Space Consultant Carole Scott

Reading Consultant
Linda B. Gambrell, Ph.D.

1 2 3 4 5 6 7 8 9 V0G1 10 09 08 07 06 05 04 03

ISBN 0-328-06204-9

The publisher would like to thank the following for their
kind permission to reproduce their photographs:
c=center; b=bottom; l=left; r=right; t=top

Genesis Space Library: 14cr; N.A.S.A.: 10cl; **Planet Earth Pictures:**
4br, 15t, 30-31; **Popperfoto:** Reuters 12br; **Science Photo Library:**
A. Sokolov & A. Leonov/ASAP 20bl; **NASA:** 6, 11, 13, 21, 23, 26cl;
Times Syndication: 7br.

All other Images © Dorling Kindersley Limited.
For further information see www.dkimages.com

dk.com

Nota para los maestros

Estos libros de *Dorling Kindersley* para primeros lectores, proporcionados a través de *Pearson Education,* han sido diseñados con la participación de destacados expertos en el campo de la lectura, como la Dra. Linda Gambrell, presidenta de la Conferencia Nacional de Lectura y ex-miembro del Consejo de la Asociación Internacional de Lectura. Los libros exploran temas de interés infantil y, asimismo, ofrecen una oportunidad de enriquecer el contenido académico de todos los grados de *Estudios sociales Scott Foresman* de una manera integral y divertida.

Las hermosas ilustraciones y fotografías a color se combinan con historias atractivas de lectura fácil y ofrecen una presentación novedosa de cada tema. Cada libro despertará el interés de los niños, y desarrollará sus destrezas de lectura, su cultura general y su amor por la lectura.

Linda es astronauta.

Viaja en el transbordador espacial.

Va a arreglar un telescopio
que se dañó.

A Linda le encanta viajar al espacio.

Es muy emocionante.

Cuando mira por la ventanilla,
ve la Tierra allá abajo.

¡Qué hermosa vista!

Ve los pueblos, los ríos
y las montañas.

Los telescopios

Con un telescopio de la Tierra vemos estrellas y planetas. Con los telescopios que están en el espacio podemos ver mucho más lejos.

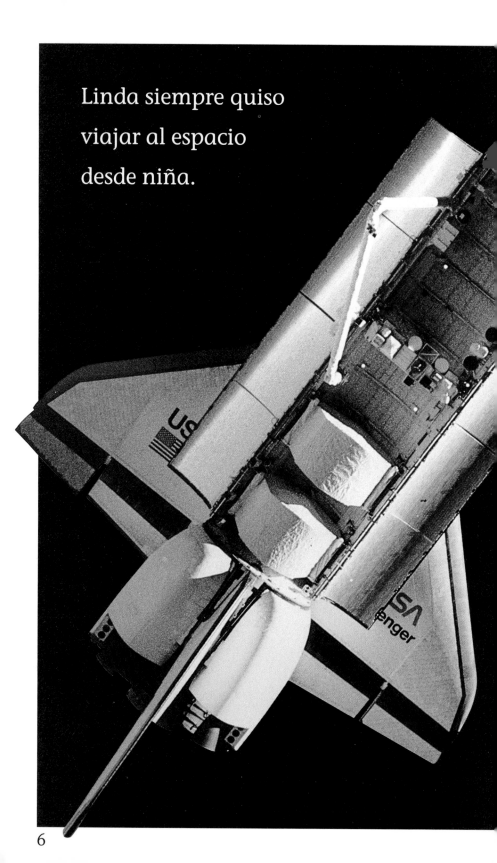

Linda siempre quiso
viajar al espacio
desde niña.

Cuando pidió trabajo
de astronauta,
miles de personas
querían el mismo trabajo.
Pero sólo había lugar
para seis personas.

A Linda le hicieron muchas pruebas.
Le examinaron el corazón,
los pulmones, la vista y los oídos.
¡Y la eligieron para el trabajo!

La ciencia en el espacio

Muchos astronautas son científicos.
Los médicos estudian lo que nos
pasa en el espacio. Los biólogos
estudian lo que les pasa a las
plantas y a los animales.

Linda se preparó 18 meses
para ser astronauta.
Con una máquina,
practicaba moverse
como si estuviera
en el espacio.

Es muy distinto
estar en la Tierra
que estar en el espacio.
En la Tierra,
una fuerza llamada
la fuerza de gravedad
nos mantiene
en el suelo.
La fuerza de gravedad
es menor en el espacio.
Los astronautas
flotan.
A esto se le llama
ingravidez.
Se debe
al movimiento
del transbordador

Antes de cada misión,

los astronautas se preparan

para la tarea que van a hacer.

Linda aprendió a arreglar

un telescopio para esta misión.

 Hizo prácticas

con un modelo

de telescopio

en una alberca

porque estar debajo

del agua se parece

a estar en el espacio.

Linda practicó mucho,

hasta que no se equivocó ni una vez.

Ahora sí podía viajar

en el transbordador espacial.

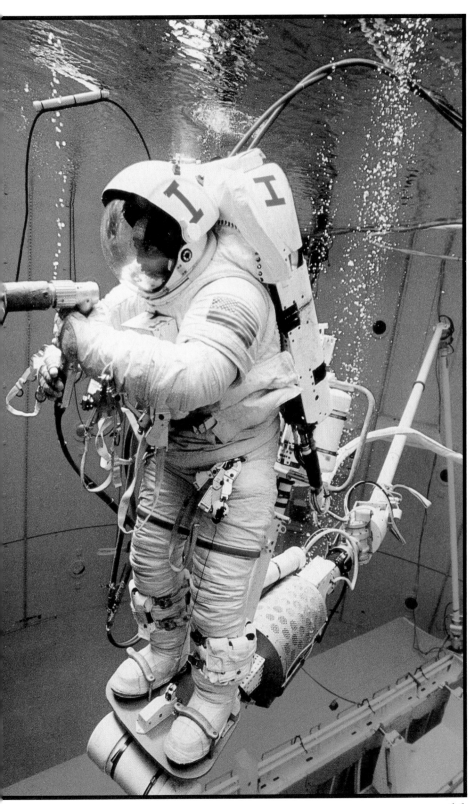

Ésta es la cuarta misión de Linda.

Linda siente nervios cuando

se abrocha el cinturón de seguridad.

Comienza la cuenta regresiva:

diez, nueve, ocho, siete, seis, cinco,

cuatro, tres, dos, uno, ¡despegue!

Se oye un

RUGIDO

ensordecedor cuando los cohetes

lanzan el transbordador

hacia el espacio.

El traje espacial

Los astronautas llevan
trajes espaciales anaranjados
para el despegue y el aterrizaje.
Estos trajes les permiten
tolerar fuerzas inusuales.

En la Tierra, miran el despegue
en el Centro de comando.
Pueden comunicarse con la tripulación
en cualquier momento.
En tan sólo
30 segundos,
el transbordador
sale del cielo azul
y entra
en la oscuridad
del espacio.

Los cohetes
y el tanque
de combustible caen al mar.
Allí los recogen
para volver
a usarlos
en otra misión.

Avistar el transbordador

A veces se puede ver un transbordador
dando la vuelta a la Tierra.
Parece
una estrella
en movimiento.

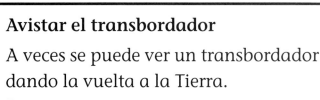

Linda se cambia de ropa

para descansar.

Los pantalones tienen bolsillos

para poner las plumas

y la comida.

Si no, flotarían.

Los transbordadores espaciales
tienen tres partes:
un avión, que se llama orbitador,
un tanque de combustible
y dos cohetes que lanzan
el orbitador al espacio.
En la bodega del orbitador
se lleva el equipo,
como un laboratorio o un telescopio.
La tripulación usa un brazo robot
para sacar y poner las cosas
en la bodega.

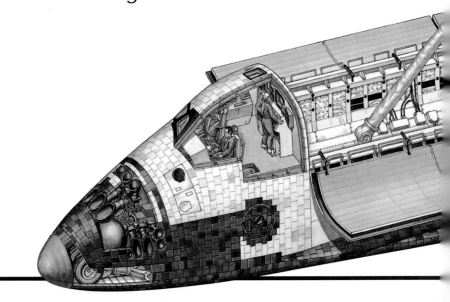

En la misión de Linda
van ocho astronautas.
Viven y trabajan en la cabina.
El comandante está a cargo
de la misión.
Se sienta junto al piloto frente
a los controles del orbitador.

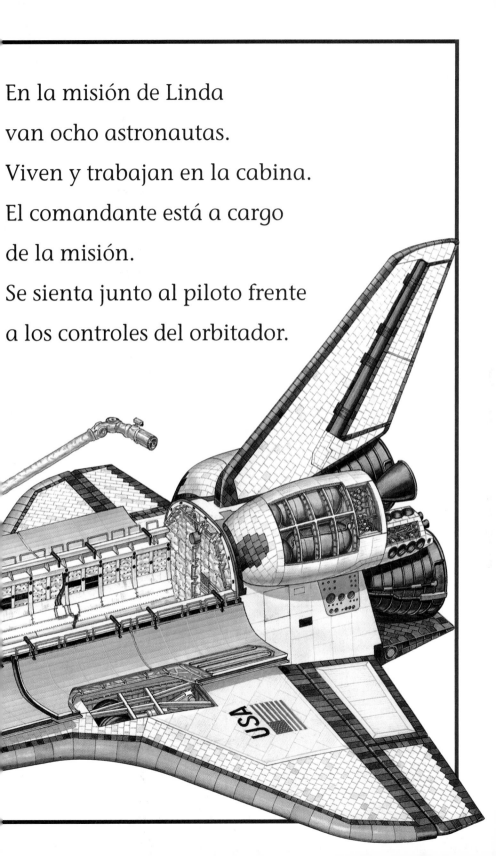

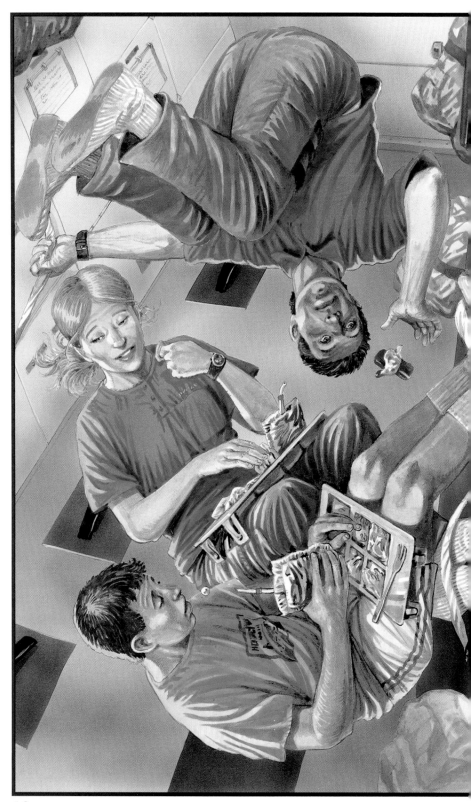

Unas horas después de despegar,
unos miembros de la tripulación
toman un descanso.

Es hora de almorzar.

Linda se abrocha el cinturón.

La comida está en paquetes
pegados a una bandeja.

Linda se amarra la bandeja a la pierna.

Come con un tenedor y una cuchara.

Pero toma la bebida con un popote
para que las gotas no floten.

Comida espacial

Hay más de 70 comidas.
Unas están listas
para comer. A otras
hay que agregarles agua.

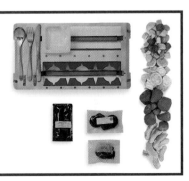

Por fin llegan al telescopio

que tienen que arreglar.

Linda se pone un traje especial

para la caminata espacial.

Este traje tiene oxígeno porque

en el espacio no hay aire.

El casco tiene auriculares

y un micrófono para que Linda

hable con la tripulación.

Lleva una mochila con propulsores

a chorro para moverse en el espacio.

La caminata espacial

El astronauta ruso
Alexei Leonov
fue la primera persona
que caminó en el espacio
en marzo de 1965.

¡Por fin está en el espacio!

Linda empieza a arreglar

el telescopio.

Pero el telescopio está doblado

y la herramienta

que Linda llevó no sirve.

Tiene que llevar el telescopio

a la bodega del orbitador

para arreglarlo allí.

Linda explica el problema

al comandante.

El comandante mueve el brazo robot

para agarrar el telescopio.

¿Alcanzará?

Linda se para sobre el brazo

y da instrucciones.

El brazo
apenas alcanza.
Linda agarra el telescopio.
El comandante lo mete
en la bodega del orbitador
con el brazo robot.

Linda demora varias horas
en arreglar el telescopio.
Después ayuda al comandante
a colocarlo de nuevo en el espacio.
Linda está contenta
porque hizo su trabajo.

Dentro del transbordador,
Linda tiene que hacer ejercicio.
Como pesa menos en el espacio
que en la Tierra,
sus huesos y músculos
no trabajan mucho.
Tiene que hacer ejercicio
dos horas al día
para no debilitarse.

Linda hace ejercicio
en una máquina.
Un médico chequea
su salud
cuando
hace ejercicio.

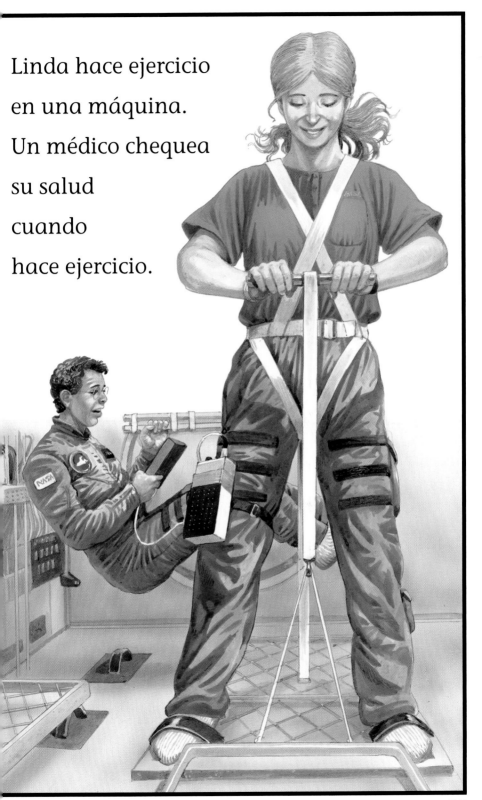

Cuando termina,

Linda se lava con toallitas húmedas.

En el transbordador no hay duchas.

Las gotas de agua

podrían flotar y dañar el equipo.

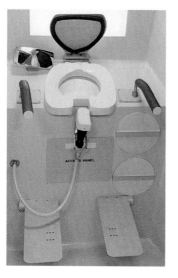

Pero sí hay un baño

que absorbe todo

para que nada se dañe.

Pronto es la hora

de dormir de Linda.

Se trepa a una litera

empotrada en la pared y se acuesta.

Los astronautas duermen por turnos,

de modo que siempre hay

unos despiertos para trabajar.

¡Es hora de regresar a la Tierra!
Esto puede ser peligroso.
La Tierra está rodeada
por una capa de gases
que se llama atmósfera.
El orbitador tiene que
atravesar la atmósfera
con el ángulo exacto.
Si el ángulo
es más grande,
el orbitador
se quema.
Si el ángulo
es más pequeño,
rebota y vuelve al espacio.
¡El orbitador atraviesa la atmósfera
con el ángulo exacto!

Linda mira por la ventanilla.

El orbitador se ve rojo brillante:

está a 2,500 °F.

Pero tiene unas baldosas
especiales para no
quemarse. De pronto,
una baldosa sale volando.

Linda no se preocupa.

Es sólo un pequeño pedazo.

El orbitador empieza

a deslizarse por el aire.

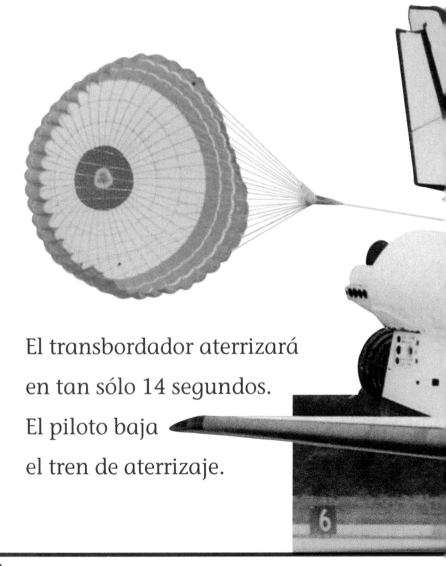

El transbordador aterrizará

en tan sólo 14 segundos.

El piloto baja

el tren de aterrizaje.

El orbitador aterriza.

Tiene un paracaídas especial

para ir más despacio.

Los astronautas tienen que esperar

a que el orbitador se enfríe.

Por fin pueden salir.

Linda mira hacia el espacio.

Ya está deseando embarcarse

en otra misión.

Datos sobre el espacio

En el espacio, los astronautas miden hasta tres cuartos de pulgada más de altura que en la Tierra.

El corazón puede debilitarse en el espacio porque no tiene que trabajar tanto como en la Tierra.

Dentro del transbordador hay que hacer circular oxígeno para que los astronautas puedan respirar.

Los astronautas beben el vapor de agua de su propia respiración después de reciclarlo.

Si un astronauta quiere afeitarse, tiene que aspirar los pelillos antes de que salgan flotando.

Los astronautas usan una computadora portátil para comunicarse con familiares y amigos desde el espacio.

Una vez el despegue de un transbordador se demoró porque un pájaro carpintero hizo 75 agujeros en el tanque de combustible.

El primer ser vivo que nació en el espacio fue una perdiz.

Susan B. Anthony

A Photo-Illustrated Biography
by Lucile Davis

Content Consultant:
Andrea Libresco
Department of Curriculum and Teaching
Hofstra University

Bridgestone Books
an imprint of Capstone Press

Facts about Susan B. Anthony

- Susan B. Anthony was a leader in the fight for women's rights.
- Elizabeth Cady Stanton was another women's rights leader. Susan met Elizabeth in 1851. They worked together for 51 years.
- In 1872, police arrested Susan for trying to vote. At the time, women were not allowed to vote.

Bridgestone Books are published by Capstone Press
151 Good Counsel Drive, P.O. Box 669 Mankato, Minnesota 56002
www.capstonepress.com

052011   006169R

Library of Congress Cataloging-in-Publication Data
Davis, Lucile.
Susan B. Anthony: a photo-illustrated biography/by Lucile Davis.
    p. cm.--(Read and discover photo-illustrated biographies)
    Includes bibliographical references (p. 24).
    Summary: An introductory biography of the early women's rights activist who fought for
women's right to vote.
    ISBN-13: 978-1-56065-750-7 (hardcover)   ISBN-10: 1-56065-750-2 (hardcover)
    ISBN-13: 978-0-7368-8422-8 (softcover pbk.)   ISBN-10: 0-7368-8422-X (softcover pbk.)
    1. Anthony, Susan B. (Susan Brownell), 1820-1906--Juvenile literature. 2. Feminists--United States--Biography--
Juvenile literature. 3. Suffragists--United States--Biography--Juvenile literature. 4. Women--Suffrage--United
States--History--Juvenile literature. [1. Anthony, Susan B. (Susan Brownell), 1820-1906. 2. Feminists. 3. Women--
Biography.] I. Title. II. Series.
HQ1413.A55D38 1998
305.42'092--dc21
[B]   97-41651
                                                                                        CIP
                                                                                        AC

Editorial Credits
Editor, Greg Linder; cover design, Timothy Halldin; photo research, Michelle L. Norstad

Photo Credits
Archive Photos, cover, 4, 10; Corbis-Bettmann, 8, 12, 16, 20; Department of Rare Books and Special
Collections, University of Rochester Library, 6; Schlesinger Library, Radcliffe College, 14, 18

Table of Contents

Leader and Guide

Susan Brownell Anthony was an American women's rights leader. She guided the struggle for women's rights in the 1800s. She believed women should have the same rights as men.

Susan was a Quaker. Quakers are members of a Christian group founded in 1650. Christians are people who follow the teachings of Jesus Christ. Quakers oppose all war. They believe that men and women should be treated equally.

Both men and women spoke at Quaker meetings in the 1800s. Only men could speak at most churches.

At that time, women could not vote. They could not hold government offices. Married women could not own property or sue people in court. Most colleges would not accept women as students.

Susan knew this was not fair. She met other women who felt the same way. She spent most of her life working for women's rights.

Susan B. Anthony spent her life working for women's rights.

Early Years

Susan B. Anthony was born February 15, 1820, in Adams, Massachusetts. Her father Daniel ran a cotton mill. Her mother Lucy raised eight children. Susan's father was a Quaker. Her mother was not. Susan became a Quaker at age 13.

Susan learned to read and write by the age of five. She wanted to learn math. The school master would not teach math to girls. So Susan taught herself.

Susan's father hired young women to work in his mill. Many of the women stayed at the Anthony home. They worked 12 hours a day. Susan's mother worked even longer. She cooked and cleaned for the family during the day. At night, she cooked for the women who worked at the mill.

Susan helped her mother. She could cook an entire dinner by the age of ten. She understood that running a household was hard work.

Susan became a Quaker like her father Daniel.

School Teacher

Susan's father believed education was important. Daniel taught classes for the mill workers at night. He sent Susan to an advanced school for girls. She was 17. But Daniel's business failed a year later.

Susan became a teacher to help support her family. She taught at a school in New York.

In 1846, Susan became the head teacher for girls. The head teacher for boys at the school was a man. He earned more money than Susan because he was a man. She knew this was not fair. But she did not know what to do about it.

Susan's parents attended a women's rights meeting in 1850. They told Susan about laws that were unfair to women. A year later, Susan decided to quit teaching. Instead, she would work to change unfair laws. She started working for women's rights.

Susan quit teaching in 1851. She started working to change laws that were unfair to women.

Susan Meets Elizabeth

Susan met Elizabeth Cady Stanton in 1851. Elizabeth had planned the first women's rights convention in 1848. A convention is a meeting of people with the same interests. The women's rights convention took place in Seneca Falls, New York.

Susan and Elizabeth became friends for life. They made a good team. Susan was a good speaker and a good planner. Elizabeth was a powerful speaker and writer. They started working to win equal rights for women.

Elizabeth made speeches and wrote articles. Her words helped people understand the need for women's rights. Susan set up meetings. Her plans guided people in their work.

Elizabeth was married. She was also busy raising seven children. She could not be away from home very often. Susan never married. She could travel freely and speak about women's rights.

Susan (right) and Elizabeth Cady Stanton (left) became friends for life.

A Petition for Rights

Susan and Elizabeth created a petition in 1854. A petition is a letter signed by many people. Petitions often ask for changes in the law. Ten thousand people signed Susan and Elizabeth's petition.

Susan and Elizabeth presented their petition to the New York legislature. A legislature is a group of people that makes laws. The petition asked legislators to give women equal rights.

Elizabeth gave a powerful speech. Most legislators respected what she had to say. But they did not do what the women asked. Susan told the legislators she would be back.

Susan returned to the legislature with more petitions. In 1860, legislators finally passed a new law. It gave married women in New York the right to own property. Single women already had that right. Women still did not have the same rights as men. But the new law was a beginning.

This cartoon shows Elizabeth speaking to the New York legislature. She asked legislators to give women equal rights.

Slavery and Equal Rights

Susan and Elizabeth also fought against slavery. They believed that no one should own another person. They started a women's group to help end slavery.

Susan created another petition. About 400,000 people signed this petition. Susan presented it to the United States Congress in 1864. Congress makes laws for the entire country.

Congress passed the 13th Amendment to the U.S. Constitution in 1865. An amendment is a change made to a law. The 13th Amendment ended slavery in the United States. Susan's petition helped Congress decide to pass the amendment.

Congress passed the 14th Amendment in 1868. It granted rights to men who were once slaves. But these men could not vote. Women did not have the right to vote either. Susan and Elizabeth began working to win equal rights for all people.

Susan's petition helped Congress decide to end slavery.

The Revolution

In 1868, Susan and Elizabeth started a newspaper. It was called *The Revolution.*

Articles in the newspaper explained the need for equal rights. Susan and Elizabeth also printed articles about other subjects. They printed articles about education, business, marriage, and women's history.

Susan raised money to print the newspaper. Elizabeth wrote many articles. As many as 3,000 readers paid to receive the newspaper.

Congress passed the 15th Amendment to the U.S. Constitution in 1870. It gave African-American men the right to vote. The amendment did not give women this right. Many women were disappointed.

Susan and Elizabeth stopped printing *The Revolution* in 1870. The newspaper owed $10,000 to printers and other people. Susan promised to pay the $10,000 with her own money. She finished paying six years later.

Susan (right) and Elizabeth (left) started a newspaper called *The Revolution.*

Woman Suffrage

Susan traveled across the United States. She gave speeches about the need for woman suffrage. Suffrage is the right to vote.

Susan decided to break the law by voting in 1872. A police officer arrested her. In court, a judge fined her $100. Susan refused to pay the fine. Instead, she gave a speech about woman suffrage.

Susan and Elizabeth wrote three books about woman suffrage. The first book was published in 1881. It was called *A History of Woman Suffrage.*

In 1888, Susan planned a meeting for women from many nations. Women came to the United States from Europe and Asia. The meeting helped bring worldwide attention to women's rights.

Susan and Elizabeth became leaders of a woman suffrage group. Elizabeth was president. Susan guided the work of the group. Susan continued leading the group after Elizabeth died in 1902.

Susan planned a meeting for women from many nations in 1888.

The 19th Amendment

In 1906, Susan spoke at a national woman suffrage meeting. She asked women to keep working for the right to vote. Susan died one month later.

Susan had prepared other women to work for women's rights. They took up the fight. In 1920, the 19th Amendment was passed. Many people called this law the Susan B. Anthony Amendment. The 19th Amendment gave women the right to vote.

An artist named Adelaide Johnson created a statue. The statue shows Elizabeth, Susan, and Lucretia Mott. Lucretia was another women's rights leader. The artist gave the statue to the United States in 1921. It now stands in the Capitol building in Washington, D.C. The statue honors the women who worked for equal rights.

The U. S. government honored Susan many years later. The government put her picture on a coin. The Susan B. Anthony dollar first appeared in 1979.

Artist Adelaide Johnson created this statue of Elizabeth, Susan, and Lucretia Mott.

Words from Susan B. Anthony

"Still another form of slavery remains to be disposed of; the old idea yet prevails that woman is owned and possessed by man."

From a speech by Susan B. Anthony. She spoke in Kansas at the close of the Civil War.

"The most ignorant and degraded man who walks to the polls feels himself superior to the most intelligent woman."

From a speech, 1894

"Failure is impossible."

A statement Susan made at her 86th birthday party. She believed women could not fail if they kept working for women's rights.

"Men, their rights and nothing more.
Women, their rights and nothing less."

Motto of *The Revolution,* the newspaper started by Susan and Elizabeth Cady Stanton.

Important Dates in Susan B. Anthony's Life

1820—Born February 15 in Adams, Massachusetts

1838—Becomes a school teacher to help support her family

1851—Meets Elizabeth Cady Stanton

1854—Presents a petition for women's rights to the New York state legislature

1864—Presents a petition opposing slavery to the U.S. Congress

1868—Starts a newspaper called *The Revolution*

1872—Is arrested after voting

1902—Susan's friend Elizabeth Cady Stanton dies

1906—Susan dies in Rochester, New York

Words to Know

amendment (uh-MEND-muhnt)—a change made to a law

Christian (KRISS-chun)—a follower of the teachings of Jesus Christ

Congress (KONG-griss)—the part of the U.S. government that makes laws for the whole country

convention (kuhn-VEN-shun)—a meeting of people with the same interests

legislature (LEJ-iss-lay-chur)—a group of people that makes laws

petition (puh-TISH-uhn)—a letter signed by many people

Quaker (KWAY-kur)—a member of a Christian group founded in 1650

suffrage (SUF-ruhj)—the right to vote

Read More

Harvey, Miles. *Women's Voting Rights*. Cornerstones of Freedom. Danbury, Conn.: Children's Press, 1996.

Kendall, Martha E. *Susan B. Anthony: Voice for Women's Voting Rights*. Historical American Biographies. Springfield, N.J.: Enslow, 1997.

Parker, Barbara Keevil. *Susan B. Anthony: Daring to Vote*. A Gateway Biography. Brookfield, Conn.: Millbrook Press, 1998.

Useful Addresses and Internet Sites

FactHound offers a safe, fun way to find Internet sites related to this book. All of the sites on FactHound have been researched by our staff.

Here's how:
1. Visit *www.facthound.com*
2. Choose your grade level.
3. Type in this book ID **1560657502** for age-appropriate sites. You may also browse subjects by clicking on letters, or by clicking on pictures and words.
4. Click on the **Fetch It** button.

FactHound will fetch the best sites for you!

Index